T5-AFT-761

BEARDED DRAGONS

by Jaclyn Jaycox

PEBBLE
a capstone imprint

Pebble Explore is published by Pebble, an imprint of Capstone.
1710 Roe Crest Drive
North Mankato, Minnesota 56003
www.capstonepub.com

**Library of Congress Cataloging-in-Publication data is available on
the Library of Congress website.**
ISBN 978-1-9771-2312-1 (library binding)
ISBN 978-1-9771-2646-7 (paperback)
ISBN 978-1-9771-2320-6 (eBook PDF)

Summary: Text describes bearded dragons, including where they live, their
bodies, what they do, and dangers to bearded dragons.

Image Credits
Capstone Press, 6; Dreamstime: Marcel Klimko, 13, Naturesauraphoto,
10, Serena Livingston, 15, Smileitsmccheeze, 25; Newscom: Steimer, C./
picture alliance / Arco Images G, 19; Science Source: ANT Photo Library,
22; Shutterstock: Ashley Whitworth, 8, Camilo Torres, 17, Cre8tive Images,
Cover, Egoreichenkov Evgenii, 18, Ery Azmeer, 14, Frank Kebschull, 24,
kurthiggins74, 5, lessysebastian, 21, Ryan Ladbrook, 28, StartNow, 1,
stockfotoart, 7, Vaclav Sebek, 11; SuperStock: NHPA, spread 26-27

Editorial Credits
Editor: Mandy Robbins; Designer: Dina Her; Media Researcher:
Morgan Walters; Production Specialist: Tori Abraham

All internet sites appearing in back matter were available and accurate
when this book was sent to press.

Printed in the United States of America.
PA117

Table of Contents

Words in **bold** are in the glossary.

Amazing Bearded Dragons

Do bearded dragons have wings and fly? Do they breathe fire? No! Bearded dragons are not like dragons from stories. They are a type of **reptile**. Their skin has scales. They lay eggs.

Reptiles are **cold-blooded**. They can't control their body heat. If it's cold outside, they are cold. If it's hot, they are hot.

There are eight different kinds of bearded dragons. They are very gentle. Many people keep them as pets.

Where in the World

Bearded dragons are found in Australia. They live in warm **habitats**. They wander around hot deserts. They also live in woodlands and flat, grassy areas called **savannas**.

Bearded Dragons Range Map

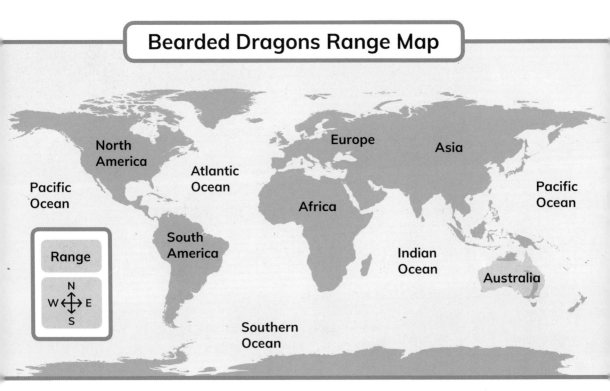

North America

Europe

Asia

Pacific Ocean

Atlantic Ocean

Pacific Ocean

Africa

Range

South America

Indian Ocean

N
W←✦→E
S

Australia

Southern Ocean

Bearded dragons spend a lot of time in the sun. They lay on rocks. They need the heat. It keeps them warm. Sometimes it gets too hot. They **burrow** underground to stay cool.

Bearded Dragon Bodies

Bearded dragons are rough and bumpy. They are covered in scales. They have soft spikes along their sides. They have them on their heads and throats too. The spikes get hard when bearded dragons are scared. Spikes protect them from **predators** that attack them.

A bearded dragon can puff out its throat. Its neck darkens. It looks like a beard. That's how bearded dragons got their name. They do this to scare animals away. Their beards make them look bigger.

Bearded dragons can weigh up to
1.1 pounds (0.5 kilograms). They grow
up to 24 inches (61 centimeters) long
from head to tail. Their tails are usually
as long as their bodies.

Some bearded dragons are tan. Others are brown. They may have a little red or gold mixed in. Their skin can change colors. They turn darker to soak up more heat. They lighten to cool off.

A bearded dragon has a triangle-shaped head. The scales on its head help it drink. When it rains, water gathers on a bearded dragon's head. It runs down the scales right to its mouth.

Bearded dragons have short legs. Their bodies are wide. They are not fast runners. But they are great climbers. They climb trees to escape predators.

Bearded dragons have eyes on the sides of their heads. They can see all around. They have great hearing too. You have to look closely to spot their ears. They are the two holes on their heads!

Bearded dragons don't have to chase **prey**. They use their sticky tongues to grab food! Strong jaws help them chew crunchy insects. Their front teeth bite and tear prey. These teeth fall out and grow back many times. Their side teeth chew plants.

On the Menu

A bearded dragon sits high up in a tree. It looks at a branch below. It spots a tasty treat. A bug is walking along the branch. The bearded dragon quietly climbs down. It sneaks up behind the bug. It sticks out its tongue and grabs it. Chomp!

Bearded dragons eat many kinds of bugs and worms. They eat plant leaves and flowers too. Sometimes they eat fruit.

Bigger animals are on the menu too. Bearded dragons eat mice and small lizards. When bearded dragons bite their prey, they let out **venom**. It kills the prey.

Food can be hard to find in the desert. Bearded dragons eat many different foods. They eat large meals when they can. They might not find more food for a few days.

Life of a Bearded Dragon

Bearded dragons are most active in the spring and summer. During winter there is less sunlight. The weather gets colder. They sleep more then. They save **energy**.

Bearded dragons send each other messages. Males will bob their heads at smaller males. This shows they are bigger and stronger. The smaller one might wave to agree. Or he may bob his head to show he wants to fight. Males also bob their heads and wave their legs to attract females.

Bearded dragons usually live alone. They come together to **mate**. They mate in the spring and summer.

Females dig a burrow. They lay their eggs in it. They can lay more than 20 eggs at a time. A group of eggs is called a **clutch**. Females can lay up to nine clutches a year. The eggs hatch about two months later.

Baby bearded dragons are called hatchlings. They are about 4 inches (10 cm) long. The mother doesn't care for them. They are able to take care of themselves. They eat small insects.

Young bearded dragons shed every few weeks. They get rid of old skin. New skin grows. They grow bigger. They shed many times. At two years old, they are fully grown. Adults shed only twice a year. They can live up to 10 years in the wild.

Dangers to Bearded Dragons

Bearded dragons have many predators. Birds, snakes, and large lizards try to eat them. Wild dogs and foxes hunt them too.

People are the biggest danger to bearded dragons. People clear land for cattle farming. They build roads and buildings. They cut down trees and bushes. Bearded dragons are losing their homes.

Bearded dragons are popular pets. In the past, too many were being taken from the wild. They were sold as pets. Australia now has laws against this. People cannot take bearded dragons from the wild.

Fast Facts

Name: bearded dragon

Habitat: deserts, savannas, woodlands

Where in the World: Australia

Food: plants, bugs, worms, fruit, small lizards, mice

Predators: birds, snakes, large lizards, wild dogs, foxes

Life span: up to 10 years

Glossary

burrow (BUHR-oh)—to dig a hole; a burrow can also be a hole in the ground that an animal makes

clutch (KLUHCH)—a group or nest of eggs

cold-blooded (KOHLD-BLUH-duhd)—having a body that needs to get heat from its surroundings

energy (E-nuhr-jee)—the strength to do active things without getting tired

habitat (HAB-uh-tat)—the home of a plant or animal

mate (MATE)—to join together to produce young

predator (PRED-uh-tur)—an animal that hunts other animals for food

prey (PRAY)—an animal hunted by another animal

reptile (REP-tile)—a cold-blooded animal that breathes air and has a backbone; most have scales

savanna (suh-VAN-uh)—a flat, grassy area of land with few or no trees

venom (VEN-uhm)—a liquid poison made by an animal to kill its prey

Read More

Andres, Marco. *Bearded Dragons*. New York: PowerKids Press, 2018.

Davin, Rose. *Lizards*. North Mankato, MN: Capstone Press, 2017.

Mara, Wil. *Bearded Dragons*. North Mankato, MN: Capstone Press, 2017.

Internet Sites

Bearded Dragon Facts for Kids
kids.kiddle.co/Bearded_dragon

Bearded Dragon Facts & Worksheets
kidskonnect.com/animals/bearded-dragon/

Lizard
animals.sandiegozoo.org/animals/lizard

Index